One Day You Will Tell Me

Collected Poems

by
Irma Kurti

One Day You Will Tell Me

Collected poems by
Irma Kurti

One Day You Will Tell Me

By Irma Kurti

First Edition

Author: Irma Kurti
Editor: Paul Gilliland
Formatting: Southern Arizona Press
Cover Photograph by Biagio Fortini

Published by Southern Arizona Press
Sierra Vista, Arizona 85635
www.SouthernArizonaPress.com

ISBN: 978-1-960038-09-8

Poetry

Dedication

To my parents, Hasan Kurti and Sherife Mezini,to tell them that there is not a single day when I don't think about them and that they are inside me, in the safest place, the soul, where only the greatest loves are preserved…

Preface

For years, I have followed the poetic activity of Irma Kurti with inexhaustible interest and great curiosity. Engaging with Kurti has granted me the opportunity to express myself over time. For me, it is a renewed honor to be able to open the precious pages of a new book written by her. Each is so full of life, emotions, and images that look with great passion at a past that is increasingly receding from the liquid everyday life.

Hers is a poetic attention to the particularities of situations and images that have the potential to bring back vivid memories. They are pleasant to remember, like a breeze of fresh air, but at the same time painful because they reveal our distance from that Edenic and carefree yesterday, which was lived in the fullness of feelings and in the company of loving figures, such as the parents to whom this collection is dedicated.

If it is true that a feeling of deep melancholy and painful expectation predominates (albeit an illusory one), these compositions are also the preferred means by which the Poetess—even today—can keep alive that bond with her loved ones. They are indissoluble presences in her existence that inhabit every domain of her experience in an omnipresent way.

As already observed elsewhere, the image of one's own parents is formed not only in the moments of serenity in which they were limited to an age of happiness, when life flowed normally without particular worries, but also in the bitterest moments. The Poetess recalls the latter with a mixture of sadness and resentment, as in the lyric dedicated to her beloved mother: "*And the roads extended before you / without end and beginning*

/ as in the twilight, you tried to collect / the last pieces of your desires that vanished / just like some white clouds." Poetry itself becomes a feeling of time and is gradually colored with images of torment due to the affliction of the pain felt by her ill parents, with gasps of escape and the desire to hope, but also with careful descriptions of environments, circumstances, and the changing times and seasons. The whole work profoundly evokes the changes of time, its unstoppable evasion that makes us discover fragile, transient beings in constant evolution subjected to the inclement human weather of detachment, mourning, and absence. These are moments—to cite Van Gennep—in which the humans consciously elaborate the passage from one stage to another and in which the liminary frontier areas frequently represent experiences of gloom and confusion, lived in an excruciating loneliness and a frantic search for reasons that, unfortunately, cannot be identified.

However, the book presents a wide thematic variety, which makes it enjoyable and persuasive to the reader. We rediscover the feeling of nostalgia for the homeland (*"As I dream of rinsing my body / there where the waterfall flows,"* and again, "*We had the sea close by, it didn't take much / to hold the waves in our hands*") but also get a look at the canonical existential vexations that situate humans in insurmountable aporias and impracticable dilemmas ("*Who will accompany you in a dream, / [...] when I won't be any more in this life?"*).

The Poetess also reflects on the authentic value of the word and the ease of *saying*, which often reveals hypocritical verbal constructions ("*no one believes in their words /even those who wrote them*")—a sign of a reality in which there is an irremediable gap between meaning and signifier and in which incommunicability and sloppiness, even within the world of feelings, which should be ardently protected, seem to take lead roles. All this is contrasted with a timeless, metaphysical language made up of sounds perceived in the interior, of unspoken dialogues and perceptions that bring the Poetess closer to her loved ones—a sort of imperceptible ultrasound who strengthens, albeit in silence, a bond of love that never faded, not even with death *("The power of your thought will take me to you / to make all sadness vanish")*. Irma Kurti, who is a poetess inscribed in the etymological history of the word "poetry," shows herself to be an attentive and passionate woman when writing on paper, thanks to her brilliant attitude and the creative spark that propels her. Images, shapes, and changes fascinate us: *"I collect streams of rain / in my hands like small / ponds and transform / lightning into lamps / to illuminate your road / when you come back to me."*

LORENZO SPURIO
Poet and Literary Critic

Contents

Red Roses

The red roses have been cut
for they were wild, did not
disperse scent at all. There's
nothing left now, only a few
branches that, like arms, seek
help. The scattered buds on
the grass are wet with dew.
The petals thrown here and
there wait full of hope that
someone will take and hold
them in the palm, smell them,
give another, the last chance,
in the end, wake them from
the oblivion wherein they lie.

The Necklace

Don't shed tears in front of people
who consider them raindrops that
flood their roads—people who can't
feel your sorrow, the ones that go
away not to sadden themselves.

Tears now roll down your cheeks,
and slowly, they reach your neck,
forming the most beautiful necklace,
so clear, limpid, and transparent.

Let Me Go

Let me go before it's too late towards
a land where there is light and a lot
of sun, to virgin beaches without
a trace, where a wave kisses me with
passion, and a shell has the shape of a heart.

Let me go before this feeling drowns
me in an immense, turbulent ocean,
before I rest suspended on the wings
of the wind, just like an autumn leaf.

Leave, run away on any day with a
suitcase full of unspoken words, with
the gestures we have not exchanged,
with our glances full of tears and joy.

Let me go before it is too late!

I Loved You

I loved you like one loves life:
with joy and cheerfulness,
but above all, with suffering,
nostalgia, and sleepless nights.

I looked for your portrait in every
rose petal, in every clear mirror of
water. I looked for your anger in
a winter sea, for your voice in the
deep silences, and for your smile
in a distant and colorful rainbow.

Now I'm left with the crumbled
letters of your name between my
fingers, with a story, ours, which
may or may not be over, with my
spirit cracked because of the long
waits, with my slow steps from
the fear of falling once again.

And I'm still waiting for you with
hundreds of wrinkles scattered on
my skin, my gaze wet with tears,
my soul full of light, as clear as a
dewdrop that will dream about
you up to the end of days, in love.

Loneliness

It's so long, the day without you,
and it drags itself like a snake;
it crosses my existence, and so
my hours are poisoned and sad.

The sun is pale; the colors have
lost all their nuances, and behind
the windowpane I wait for you,
I look for you, I call your name
but it is all in vain.

Loneliness holds my face and
voice; it also holds your name,
whereas the light reveals like a
giant mirror my sorrow and pain.

Your Anger

I also love your anger,
the voice that rises like
a kite in the sky when
my silences remain the
best way to keep us
together and even a
laugh is too much.

I also love your anger.
It arrives after days
of light and of joy, too;
it overwhelms me like
a wave. But even then,
I imagine escaping to
a happy island without
people, only with you.

Walking on the sand,
wrapped in the magic
of the silence, hand in
hand, in love with the
breeze and the wind,
but more with your
tracks on the virgin
beaches in the long
season of winter.

I love your anger.

Irma Kurti

This Evening

This evening is beautiful, magical
like this: silent, speechless, with a
thousand stars that turn on and, in
a hurry, go out in the sky, with the
lamps on the trees imitating their light.

And I wander with your handsome
portrait in my mind, with my soul
that fills up with sounds, smiles, and
memories chased from the stars,
getting lost in another time and
a different space, where I await
your return with mixed joy and anxiety.

A Desert

How can I love you if you offer me
only this immense and deep silence
like a boundless desert burning my
soul? I wander disoriented in these
streets, surrounded by questions that
find no answer at all.

And I feel lost. It would be enough
to hear only one word from you. I
would have encoded all your fears,
your insecurities, all those doubts
that keep you away from me. One
word would be enough for me to
cross this desert: huge and infinite.

Time to Get Back

It's time to get back to my days.
It's been a century since you
knocked on my door. I do not
want to tell you anything about
my sleepless nights, those long
hours wrapped in melancholy,
how many times I stepped on
the subtle path of madness.

It's time to get back to me, to
my gray days, and to wake me
up from lethargic sleep, erase
my anxieties with your smile,
and throw a ray of sunshine
in my life. I'll be able to turn
it into the most vivid rainbow.

These are Not Leaves

These are not leaves that the autumn
throws on my hair, my shoulders;
they are hands greeting me today
while I drag an old and heavy suitcase
that keeps the seasons we lived together.

These are not raindrops running down
my cheeks, but tears: so limpid and clear.

These are not puddles reflecting now my
face but rivers of thoughts and reflections.

Goodbyes always hurt; they leave you
bitter in the heart, even if, somewhere
out there, a world of magic colors waits…

Think About Me

Think about me on your long walks
on the seashore, when the breeze is
caressing your gray hair and the sea's
salty smell rests on your skin like a tattoo.

Think about me in the long hours of
solitude under the sky embroidered
with thousands of stars, when the
cigarette trembles on your lips, the
smoke covers your face; the world
without me in it is no longer
a paradise. In those instants, when
you touch the shells that leave a
sand grain between your fingers,
when the sun sets below your look:
sweet, melancholic, lost somewhere.

The power of your thought will take
me to you to make all sadness vanish.
I will be there, by your side, to wrap
myself in your embrace as in a soft,
delicate, immense white cloud.

In the Mirror

I don't know what this thought or feeling is.
Maybe it's nothing, just a bit of drunkenness
from this spring that I live within these walls,
where the seasons don't knock to greet me.

I don't know what this emotion is; maybe it's
a crumb, maybe a world ... a need of my soul,
eager and thirsty for some harmony and love.
For the first time, in the mirror, I see my smile.

The Telephone Wire

Today I touched with my hand your
fragility, your delicate, vibrant voice
in a background of suffocated words
as if they came from another world.

And the telephone wire transmitted
everything: your unhappiness, your
agony. You were lost in sobs and in
tears telling me your gloomy story.

It transmitted everything, but not my
discomfort and sorrow, my love that
vibrated like the flash of a lighthouse
in a sea of strong waves and storms.

Other People, Other Stories

I have to meet other people, listen
to other stories, dry other tears, but
no one of them are like you, like
your tears and melodious voice.

Other people and a thousand stories
keep me stuck on the tortuous
roads. I would never like to step on
them: a chaos of events or intrigues
just like a house of cobwebs.

I have to meet other people, listen
to other stories, dry other tears too,
though inside me, I keep a gray sky
and all roads lead me back to you.

Ice Between My Fingers

I wanted to hear your voice.
My heart would blossom like
a flower; my joy would flow
just like a stream through the
long telephone wire.

I would bring the spring into
my hands, bird songs, a wealth
of buds. I would watch this
scary and chaotic world with
happy and loving eyes.

I wanted to hear your voice
and touch happiness with
my hands, but they feel cold,
so between my fingers
I now have only ice and frost.

Come Back to Me!

Come back to me if you're
not happy, if your days are
lonely, if the four walls of
your house don't make you happy.

Storms split the skies, and
the lightning is the only
neon that illuminates the
paths; drops of rain beat
now on the roof, imitating
the knocks at the door.
Come back to me tonight!

I collect streams of rain
in my hands like small
ponds and transform
lightning into lamps
to illuminate your road
when you come back to me.

The Streets of Sunday

The streets of Sunday are long and infinite;
your footprints aren't seen anywhere. The
parks, the trees are wrapped in full silence,
the branches bend over me—just like arms.

I seek your portrait under a sky that now
shows to me a veil of clouds, or on the bleak
streets, without even anonymous people or
children's smiles. It gets confused in the fog
of my immense nostalgia, of the emptiness
that I feel, and it then turns into a memory.

The streets of Sunday, infinite tracks, more
lonely and abandoned than me.

I Don't Want to Donate to You this World

I don't want to donate to you this world in ruins,
where you find violence, horror, tears of dew
and broken branches that stand in our way.

I don't want to donate to you this world in ruins,
but a part of my soul, where a song, a flower
have found a space, where a verse grows and
is transformed into a poem.

I don't want to donate to you this world, but only
the part of my anima that belongs to you.

One Day You Will Tell Me

One day, you'll tell me your story,
your first kiss, the tears you've shed
for a bygone love, your nostalgia
for your distant land and its paths.

One day, you'll tell me your story,
your walks and your slips, looking
for happiness, that open door that
never invited you in, the illusions,
insecurities, anxieties, intimacies.

I'll hear your voice, which always
restores peace in the chaos within
me, tremulous like a candle flame:
sweet, elusive, resembling a dream
as the stars fall beyond the window.

I shall feel sorry that I was not there
long ago, in that journey of your life
to dry your tears, gather your fears
in my hands, and dispel them like
white butterflies into the dark night.

We Had the Sea Close By

We had the sea close by; wide and infinite
in its anger, it tried hard to enter our words.
We had the sea close by; it didn't take much
to hold the waves in our hands. Only a step
would be enough, and the particles of sand
between our fingers would have penetrated.

But I had you close to my soul. The noises,
the waves vanished at sunset, a thousand
particles of sand faded, lost somewhere. It
was your voice that remained; like a cradle
it rocked me with the tenderness of a wave.

My Anima, a Feather

It was just a quick embrace, like
the elusive flight of a butterfly
brushing in an instant your hair.

It was just a warm hug inside a
body that trembled like a leaf,
that anonymous world, which
was a thousand times much
more familiar than my house.

It was nothing more than a hug,
but who knows why—in those
moments, my anima felt so light,
like a feather that ascends to the sky.

Under the Ruins

I don't remember how many cold days
this winter month has had, if it has been
snowing a lot, if the cars were stuck on
a patch of ice, if the happy children built
a snowman, if they were happier than ever.

I don't remember if roads were flooded
by heavy rain, if it then poured into the
river, if its drops hit the glass window,
if a poet dedicated a poem to the sun,
if passionate couples kissed under the
angry sky, if steps vanished in the distance.

But I remember very well how many
cloudy and rainy days I had myself,
how many limpid tears I have shed,
how many others have frozen in my
eyelids, how many times I have tried
to find myself under the ruins, so as
to breath, to stand up more determined again.

I Feel Naked

I feel naked in this rough winter,
and I tremble, weak and delicate;
people rush, no one looks at me,
I'm only anonymous to them.

Your hands don't cover me with
a blanket; they do not touch me,
do not give me warmth, whereas
you go away in a frenzied run and
don't realize that I'm really cold.

Oh, you don't see me trembling,
don't decipher my empty looks,
you see me as one who doesn't
exist; what really matters is only
your own tranquility and peace.

People Want Your Smile

People want only your smile,
even when your heart cries,
when it's immersed in grief,
when it sees no sun or light.

People want only your smile,
words that shine and spark,
while you are disintegrating
within yourself and feel that,
imperceptibly, you're dying.

Desires

I wish I could have wept off your tears,
the ones you swallowed in silence, Mom.
I wish I could have given you more love
and calmness as you looked behind the
glass window with your big eyes like a
beautiful dream. And the roads extended
before you, without end and beginning,
as in the twilight, you tried to collect the
last pieces of your desires that vanished
just like some white clouds.

I thought diseases could do nothing to
you, that you were immune to evil, to
pains, sufferings, or anxieties, that you
were strong and invincible like a rock,
that the waves wet but didn't destroy.

And now, I cry your tears of despair at
a time that a second chance can never
be given to me again.

A Veil

I don't know when I'll return
to my homeland again, I will
miss even the particles of dust
covering my thoughts as a cloud.

I'll miss the drops of water
falling from the faucet slowly
as I dream of rinsing my body
there where the waterfalls flow.

As I close the door, crumbs
of plaster fall on my shoulder
like a veil, transparent and white.

My Thoughts

Early morning.
My thoughts
wander,
disorientated,
without
knowing yet
what direction
to take.

The sun road
that radiates
colors, light
full of magic
or the alley
of a gray cloud?

Early morning.
Only the echo
of my thoughts
is heard as they
crash with one
another and
rotate as in a
game, trying
to choose
between sun
and shade.

Who Will Protect You?

Who will protect you from anxieties
when I am no longer in this universe,
who'll caress your beautiful forehead
saying, "Let's sleep, for it is late"?

Who will whisper words of comfort,
the ones that flow just like a stream,
who will give you a caress, a smile,
waking up your anima and fantasy?

Who will accompany you in a dream,
speak to you or give you a lot of love,
who will kiss you, who will touch you
when I won't be any more in this life?

The Spectacle of the Sky

It is the same light when I get up fast,
when I run towards the bus like crazy,
when it passes me by and I rest there,
just like a melancholic stain.

It's the same tree and the same people
I see every day, the same trembling of
leaves and the delicate fall of them.

But the sky shows a diverse spectacle;
sometimes it's gray, sometimes blue
or covered with a handful of clouds,
so soft and white. It often shows me
a plane that crosses it noisily, just like
a giant bird with its rigid, immovable
wings flying towards the infinite.

A Good Man

Today, a man passed away.
I saw him fighting against
his suffering, tired, weak,
lying in the bed as his body
and soul were slowly fading.

A good man passed away
while the others still talk,
laugh, and run towards
unknown destinations,
which rarely make them
meet happiness. Nature is
silent, it does not breathe,
the birds interrupt their
song, the air is sparse and
breathing is really fatiguing.
The anima of a few people,
that is, his family, vibrates
now like the guitar string.

Amid the Pains

When you smile amid the pains,
Father, it is not like a ray of sun
in a cloudy sky, nor a rainbow in
the tempest, nor a happiness or a
joy that enlightens my heart.

When you smile amid the pains
that don't leave your weak body,
I see the portrait of this life filled
with beauty and pain, light and
shade, joy and despair, and then,
my fragility turns into strength.

Motionless

Here is the rain we dreamed so long for.
We raised our heads, muttered prayers,
hoping it would arrive; it is transformed
into small streams carrying pebbles. Now
and then, you see papers or letters of love;
outdated, no one believes in their words,
even those who wrote them. And just in
this landscape, I stay motionless, wanting
one stream to take me and send me away
to a wavy lake or the sea of my home country.

Dancing with You, Dad

I would love to dance with you, Dad,
two waves that embrace each other,
follow the slow rhythm of your steps,
hum the fragment of a song and laugh.

We'll glide just like a ship on the sea,
talk for hours, like we did in the past,
touch happiness even for an instant,
dancing the waltz of a treacherous life.

I've forgotten the echo of your steps,
that guided me when I was a child,
now the fate has brought you down
to your knees, not your soul and heart.

I would love to dance with you, Dad.

Close to the Fire

Temperatures have dropped now
and snowflakes continue to fall,
the fire is burning in the hearth,
I don't know why I feel so cold.

You are fleeing in the darkness,
your footsteps are now covered
with snow, my heart calls your
name in a loud and shaky voice.

My words, like heavy stones on
you; sorrow and repentance I've
inside of me. As you leave in the
moonless night, sitting close to the
fire, I feel that my heart's freezing.

Irma Kurti

A Flower Petal

Sometimes you're so fragile, like a flower petal
that the wind whirls on the sidewalk, without
force, colorless, which assumes the nuances of
your sadness and sorrow.

Thus, you leave yourself in the hands of wind
throwing you wherever it wants, for you can't
tell it "yes" or "no."

A flower petal in the air is lifted by the storm,
just later, inert and hopeless, it lies on the road.

Dreamy Nights

There are nights that resemble
a dream; elusive as the breeze,
they inebriate you like a glass
of wine, as the rain mixes with
snow under the dim neon light.

The silence is muted into words,
his look is a beautiful mystery.
The dark vanishes in a second,
the moon seems magic, unique.

As you walk around the streets
you want to embrace the world,
do not want to turn back home,
because it can't contain your joy.

Your Portrait

I shall visit again the places
where we loved each other,
where we laughed and cried.

I'll walk slowly on the shore,
sit on a bench, contemplate
the sunset we used to watch
together. I shall collect then
pieces of dialog, memories,
embraces, kisses, and when
I shall leave, your portrait
will be reflected in my tears.

The Worst Wait

Seconds, minutes go by,
the wall clock beats like
a threat in this colorless
sunset. Tonight, I stay so
close to your bed as you
are leaving forever, Dad.

You hardly breath, don't
feel my hugs and kisses.
I listen to the final beats
of your heart or to your
pain and sighs that now
accompany your trip to
the last station. You keep
your eyes tightly closed,
with the desire to sleep,
never waking. But your
story is also mine; surely
you will be forever a part
of me. It is the worst wait
I have ever had in my life.

A Memory

You will be transformed into
a memory today, into a painful
and beautiful one. I'll feel no
longer your embrace or love.
My steps are slow, my heart
heavy as we accompany you
to the last shelter, where the
peace prevails, the sun is so
cold; on your grave, beneath
a poplar's shadow, thousand
of leaves the wind will blow.

The Immense Summer Sky

I was waiting for a sweet word that night
that would've filled my soul with light
while above us just like a field of fireflies
expanded the infinite summer sky.

I was just waiting for a caress like a soft
wave of the sea two steps away from us,
but you simply spoke and I was surely lost
in a labyrinth of episodes from your past.

Your voice trembled and mingled with
the waves; in fragments it came to me as
all my illusions vanished. It was enough
just to live the magic of that moment.

My love prevailed in the atmosphere; it
was filled with scents, manifold sounds,
close and elusive. I felt so happy, drunk,
your words wrapped in light—a distant
lighthouse in a dark and remote harbor.

Days have passed, turning into months,
the skies have changed and become
leaden and gray. The clouds announce
the tempests, but I still have above me
that immense summer sky like a field—
boundless and unattainable—of fireflies.

About the Author

Irma Kurti is an Albanian poetess, writer, lyricist, journalist, and translator. She is a naturalized Italian citizen who has been writing since she was a child. In 1980, she was honored with her first national prize on *Pionieri* magazine's 35th anniversary for her poem "To my homeland." In 1989, she won second prize in a national competition organized by Radio Tirana on the 45th anniversary of the Liberation of Albania.

All her books are dedicated to the memory of her beloved parents Hasan Kurti and Sherife Mezini, who supported and encouraged her on every step of her literary path.

Kurti has won numerous literary prizes and awards in Italy and Italian Switzerland. She was awarded the "Universum Donna" International Prize IX Edition 2013 for Literature and a lifetime nomination as an "Ambassador of Peace" by the University of Peace of Italian Switzerland. In 2020, she received the title of Honorary President of WikiPoesia, the Encyclopedia of Poetry. In 2021, she was awarded the title "Liria" (Freedom) by the Arbëreshë Community in Italy. She was awarded the "Leonardo da Vinci" and "Giacomo Leopardi" prizes by the "Chimera Arte Contemporanea" Cultural Association of Lecce.

In 2022, she was awarded the title of Mother Foundress and Lady of the Order of Dante Alighieri of the Republic of Poets. She is a jury member of several literary contests in Italy and a translator at the Ithaca Foundation in Spain.

Irma Kurti has published 26 books in Albanian, 20 in Italian, 10 in English, and two in French. She has written about 150 lyrics for adults and children. She is also the translator of 13 books by different authors and of all her own books in Italian and English.

Outside of Albania, her books have been published in the United States, Canada, France, Italy, Romania, Turkey, Kosovo, the Philippines, Cameroon, and India. She lives in Bergamo, Italy.

Previous Works

I Knew the Gray Sky

https://www.amazon.com/Knew-Gray-Sky-Irma-Kurti/dp/163382277X

Under my Blouse

https://www.amazon.com/Under-My-Blouse-Irma-Kurti/dp/1634486935

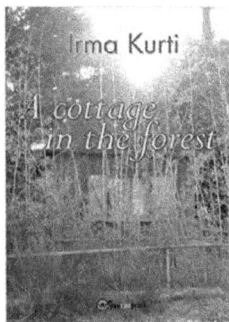

A cottage in the forest

https://www.amazon.de/-/en/Irma-Kurti/dp/8892627473

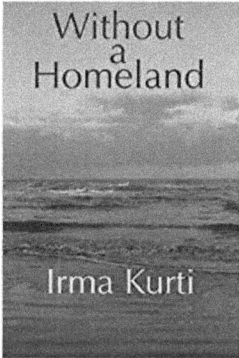

Without a Homeland

https://www.amazon.com/Without-Homeland-Irma-Kurti/dp/1946460133

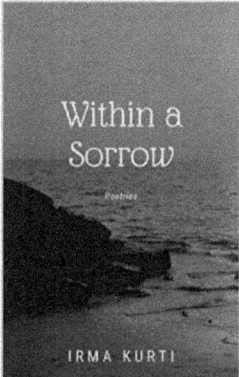

Within a Sorrow

https://www.amazon.it/Within-Sorrow-English-Irma-Kurti-ebook/dp/B09K6B543P

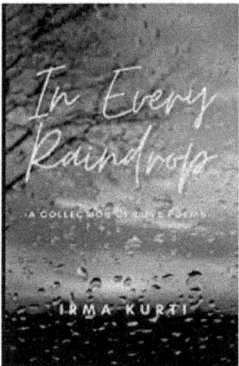

In Every Raindrop: A Collection of Love Poems

https://www.amazon.com/Every-Raindrop-Collection-Love-Poems/dp/6214701323

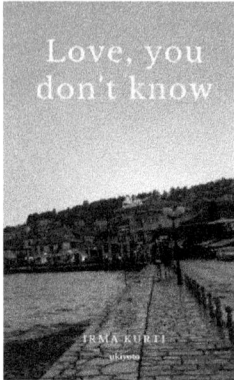

Love, you don't know

https://www.barnesandnoble.com/w/love-you-dont-know-irma-kurti/1141766631

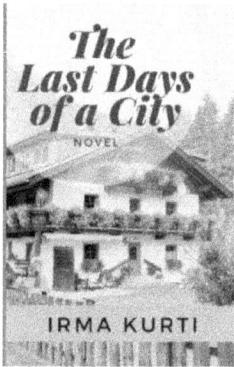

The Last Days of a City

https://www.abebooks.co.uk/book-search/author/irma-kurti/

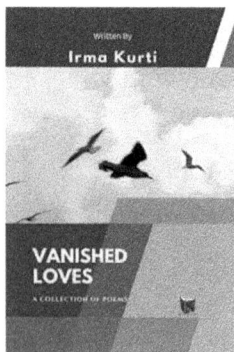

Vanished Loves: A Collection of Poems

https://www.amazon.it/Vanished-Loves-English-Irma-Kurti-ebook/dp/B0B9HSBCHS

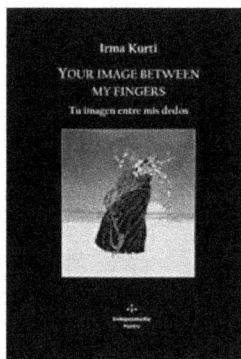

Your Image Between My Fingers: Tu imagen mis dedos

https://www.amazon.com/dp/B0BSC55Y2V

www.ingramcontent.com/pod-product-compliance
Lightning Source LLC
Chambersburg PA
CBHW071738020426
42331CB00008B/2089